Meeting God in Virtual Reality

Meeting God in Virtual Reality

Using Spiritual Practices with Media

Teresa Blythe and Daniel Wolpert

Abingdon Press
Nashville

The Convergence eBook Series

MEETING GOD IN VIRUTAL REALITY:
USING SPIRITUAL PRACTICES WITH MEDIA

Edited by Tom Bandy and Bill Easum

Copyright © 2004 by Teresa Blythe and Daniel Wolpert

This book is printed on acid-free, recycled, elemental-chlorine-free paper.

Library of Congress Cataloging-in-Publication Data

Blythe, Teresa.
  Meeting God in virtual reality : using spiritual practices with media
/ Teresa Blythe and Daniel Wolpert.
    p. cm. -- (The convergence ebook series)
  ISBN 0-687-04381-6
  1. Meditation--Christianity. 2. Mass media--Religious aspects--
Christianity. I. Wolpert, Daniel, 1959- II. Title. III. Series: Convergence
series.
  BV4813.B59 2004   /   248.3--dc22

Scripture quotations, unless otherwise noted, are from the New Revised
Standard Version of the Bible, copyright © 1989, by the Division of
Christian Education of the National Council of the Churches of Christ in
the United States of America. Used by permission.

004 05 06 07 08 09 10 11 12 13—10 9 8 7 6 5 4 3 2 1

MANUFACTURED IN THE UNITED STATES OF AMERICA

Contents

Series Foreword

Thomas G. Bandy, General Editor

Readers of the Abingdon Press *Convergence* series will welcome *Meeting God in Virtual Reality: Using Spiritual Practices with Media* by Teresa Blythe and Daniel Wolpert. There is an increasing demand for guidance that connects the explosion in contemporary media with serious disciplines of spirituality. Worship designers will not be alone in valuing this book. Spiritual directors, holistic health care professionals, and Christian educators will value the insights contained here for personal and small-group prayer and meditation.

Once again, ancient spiritual disciplines and postmodern learning methodologies have come together to offer fresh alternatives to shape lifestyle around spiritual truth. The Benedictine and Ignatian practices Teresa and Daniel describe and apply are accessible to any church participant or spiritual seeker. Their guidance helps you not only use contemporary media to enhance your spiritual life, but also go beyond the static of contemporary media to center yourself in eternal truth.

Introduction

It is instinctual for many of us to turn to prayer in the face of powerful visual images, whether we are witnessing them in person or on a screen. We have prayed while watching bombs drop in televised wars, while seeing footage of the World Trade Center towers collapse in a terrorist attack, and while viewing images of space shuttles exploding. Now is the time for us to make intentional what we have been doing intuitively all along.

Meeting God in Virtual Reality: Using Spiritual Practices with Media is for those who want to become or remain spiritually aware as they interact with television, film, music videos, recorded music, video games, and the Internet—what we are calling the world of imagined, constructed, or virtual reality.

As spiritual directors and media consumers, Teresa and Daniel not only draw understanding from their own personal and ministry experiences that God is at work within the media and entertainment culture in all its forms, but also are dedicated to drawing your attention to making this connection. Their efforts will also draw faith institutions into a more positive and interactive relationship with media.

Meeting God in Virtual Reality will link six traditional Christian spiritual disciplines to media use: the Benedictine practice of *lectio divina,* the Ignatian prayer of *examen*, discernment of the spirits, imaginative prayer, study, and even imageless centering prayer. A brief history and explanation of each practice is included, as well as easy step-by-step processes you can follow by yourself or within a group.

How to Use This Book

Each chapter refers to scenes and images from the 2001 feature film *K-PAX* for two reasons. First, since it features a sto-

ryline about an extraordinary mystery man with the power of healing and wisdom, *K-PAX* is full of religious imagery and questions, making it an excellent film to use in exploring and reflecting on spiritual themes. The film's marketing tagline is "Change the way you look at the world," and that's what this book hopes to help you do.

Second, *K-PAX* is easily accessible. It can be found at most video stores for rental and is suitable to discuss with many audiences—it is rated PG-13 for mild violence and some coarse language.

You will find references to other films and television shows as well. The examples are meant to help you see how to use these spiritual practices with media, and the step-by-step guides will allow you to use the practices with the media clip of your choice. In addition, the spiritual exercises and principles explored in this book will help you develop a greater awareness of God in all of your daily life, not just in those times you are engaged with media.

Popular culture can never fully reveal the wonder and mystery of the Divine. It does, however, shimmer with glimpses of God, if only we can cultivate, as Jesus taught Matthew 13:16, eyes to see and ears to hear. The suggestions here assist in that cultivation.

About the Authors

Teresa Blythe is a writer, spiritual director, and faith-based media literacy advocate who frequently lectures on the relationship between popular culture and spirituality. She is co-author of the 2001 Geneva Press book *Watching What We Watch: Prime-time Television Through the Lens of Faith,* and has contributed the chapter "The God of Prime-Time Television" for the 2003 Peter Lang book entitled *Religion as Entertainment.* She has written about media for *Spirituality & Health, Sojourners,* and *Presbyterians Today* and has published

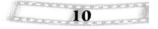

articles and essays in *The Marin Independent Journal, The Arizona Daily Star,* and *The Journal of Media and Religion.* Teresa holds a Master of Divinity and Diploma in the Art of Spiritual Direction from San Francisco Theological Seminary (2000) and has worked for more than twenty years as a broadcast journalist and media relations specialist.

The Reverend Daniel Wolpert is pastor of the First Presbyterian Church of Crookston, Minn.. Reverend Wolpert entered parish ministry in 2000 after working for many years in the mental health sector as a psychotherapist and spiritual director. He holds a Master of Divinity from San Francisco Theological Seminary (2000) and an M.A. in clinical psychology and contemplative psychotherapy from Naropa. Throughout his time in seminary, Wolpert was employed as an instructor in the Christian Spirituality Concentration at SFTS. Daniel is also the author of the 2003 Upper Room book *Creating a Life with God: The Call of Ancient Prayer Practices.*

The authors met in seminary and began a conversation about the influence of media on their own lives and spirituality. As Teresa moved into a lay ministry of media awareness and Dan began full-time parish ministry, the conversation blossomed into this book, which they hope will contribute to the groundswell of spiritual awakening taking place all over the world today.

Teresa and Daniel encourage you to share with them your experience with the prayer practices that they address in this book. Since the idea of praying with media is quite new to many people, they believe it will be beneficial to keep the conversation going. Teresa Blythe can be reached at tblythe@jps.net and the Reverend Daniel Wolpert can be reached at revdoc@gvtel.com.

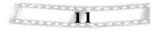

Chapter 1
Using *Lectio Divina* with Media

Your planet is really bright.
—Prot

How many times have you read a newspaper or watched a TV news story and begun to pray for the people (usually victims) involved? Perhaps as you watched a film such as *Schindler's List* you felt a deep compassion for the Jews caught up in the horror of the Holocaust, and as a result were moved to prayer. Every moment in our day is an opportunity for God's Spirit to break through to us in some way. Considering that the average American spends more than seven hours a day in front of a screen, whether it is television, computer, or film, we had better hope that God meets us in and through visual media.

One way to notice this communication is with the Christian spiritual practice known by its Latin name of *lectio divina*. This simple and traditional prayer method that has made meditation on biblical readings meaningful for so many Christians can now transform our relationship with media.

What Is *Lectio Divina*?

Lectio divina means "sacred reading." The practice of slowly reading a biblical or sacred text and allowing it to touch you with new meaning and purpose dates back to early Jewish history, in which religious leaders would pour over the scriptures in prayerful adoration. The form we know best today as *lectio divina* comes from the tradition of St. Benedict of Nursia

in the sixth century. The monastic order founded by Benedict was obedient to the *Rule of St. Benedict*, which states that members spend fixed hours of the day in prayerful reading.[1]

The practice of *lectio divina* is enjoying a newfound popularity as more people, especially Protestant and Catholic laypeople, have begun to study and appreciate a variety of Christian spiritual traditions. It also was popularized by Kathleen Norris's best-selling book, *The Cloister Walk*, in which she describes how this meditative reading transformed her life, helping her become more attentive to God and creation.[2]

When used with a written text, *lectio divina* is accessible to anyone who can read. Since it is more about listening with the heart than understanding with the mind, you do not need special training to do it. You do, however, need the capacity to slow down and savor a moment.

There are a variety of ways to do *lectio divina*, a few of which are introduced in this chapter, but primarily it consists of four steps. We will start by describing how Benedictines have used *lectio divina* with a piece of writing, usually a short passage from the Bible. For some people it may be best to experience *lectio divina* with a passage of Scripture before moving into the non-traditional use of it with media.

1. First, read *(lectio)* the short text slowly and carefully, allowing a word or phrase to gain significance for you. See if something about the passage "shimmers" or draws you to itself.

2. Enter that "shimmering" word or phrase by silently repeating it over and over. This is the ruminating phase called *meditatio*, or reflecting and meditating on what the special word or phrase may be saying to you about your life.

3. Then move into a time of silent resting with God—a phase known as *contemplatio*—in which you stay quietly open to God without asking or expecting anything.

4. Finish your session of *lectio* by observing a time of *oratio* in which you respond actively in some way to your experience of sacred reading.

In the Protestant tradition, former Augustinian monk Martin Luther (1483-1546) described his version of sacred reading in a book entitled *A Simple Way to Pray*, calling it "The Four-Stranded Garland."[3] This method recommends that the person praying with a text reflect upon a word, phrase, or image that has, for him or her, a word of instruction, thanksgiving, confession, and guidance.[4] In the exercises section, we will adapt both *lectio divina* and Luther's method for use with media.

Going Beyond the Written Word

Just because Christians have traditionally used the prayer of *lectio divina* with the written word (mostly the Bible or classic books on Christian spirituality) does not mean we are limited to the written word in this prayer. In fact, words are not mandatory for this spiritual practice; you can use it with instrumental music. Some people perform *lectio divina* on a nature walk, zeroing in on aspects of nature that draw their attention and allowing these scenes to speak to their spirit. The ancient Orthodox tradition of gazing longingly at a sacred icon in order to become closer to God is a form of sacred reading.

In this practice, the subject—be it a text, video, audio, nature, or an icon—is merely a window to communication with the

force (the Spirit of God) that speaks through creation. In *lectio divina*, that which you gaze upon does not have to be explicitly "religious." You could read a short newspaper article, watch a film clip, remember an event in your life, or listen to music. Once you learn the simple steps of reading (or paying attention), ruminating, reflecting and contemplating, and acting, you will want to use them in any number of settings.

The pivotal scene in American Beauty, when Ricky Fitts shows his girlfriend a videotape of "the most beautiful thing he has ever seen," moved me deeply, drawing me into a profound moment of awareness. In the telling of Fitts's story, while a discarded plastic bag floats and dances in front of a nondescript red brick wall, I experienced a truth about my vocation. My strongest desire, as a spiritual director, is to assist people in sifting through the experiences of their ordinary lives for evidence of God. Their stories are to me as the videotape of that plastic bag is to Ricky Fitts—ordinary on the surface but intricately beautiful and meaningful, even sacramental. I had known my vocation before I watched American Beauty, but after that scene I felt it in my bones.

I am profoundly aware of the criticism many goodhearted people show toward that scene. Some label the scene "psuedo-spirituality," but there was nothing false in that moment for me. When I hear such remarks, I sometimes wonder if I should relate this story. What makes me think I would have an experience of God while watching a videotape of a plastic bag?

And then I think, "Well, why wouldn't I experience God there?" God reaches out to us where we are the most open, and at that moment, it was in a movie theater at the hands of a team of highly creative artists. The time had come for

me to remove all barriers of where, how, and when God touches and transforms us. Thanks to the video, I can go back to that visual moment and allow it to touch me in other ways as well. I can do a "sacred reading" of it and use it as prayer.

—*Teresa*

Using *Lectio Divina* with Visual Media

First, decide what you want to pray with. It could be a film, a videotape of a favorite television program, music video or commercial (do not feel it has to be religious or even artistically significant to qualify). Narrow the selection down to a short segment that has some meaning for you. Begin with a time of silence and dedicate the experience to God. Ask God to be active in the prayer. Take your time with all of this, allowing long periods of silence between steps.

1. Watch or play your selected segment several times.

2. What attracts you most? Does anything seem to reach out to you or "shimmer" for you? It could be anything: a prop, a facial expression, a word, a phrase, or a feeling evoked by the clip. Do not censor yourself. Let your spirit be drawn to whatever it is drawn. You may also be compelled to focus on something that disturbs you. That is useful as well. Choose something that has some emotion for you. If you are watching a video and find one particular still shot that invites you into it, press the pause button and stay with it for a few minutes. Gaze at it just as one might gaze into an icon.

3. Fully enter the aspect of the clip that attracts you the

most. Is it a word, scene, sound, or emotion that speaks to you the most? Be present to it. If your mind wanders, bring it back to that image, sound, or emotion, and allow it to settle within you and deepen.

4. Reflect upon what the attracting clip may relate to in your life. Ask God to reveal that to you. What is it offering you right now?

5. Rest silently with the image, sound, or emotion. Offer it to God. Empty yourself before God, and wait on God.

6. As you prepare to end this session, what would you like to express to God about the experience of this image, sound, phrase, or word? Perhaps you would like to write about it, share it with someone, or return to it again sometime.

7. Thank God for whatever you received in this time of prayer.

This kind of prayer is especially meaningful in groups. If you are involved in a spirituality (Or just "spiritual"?) or prayer group, suggest using a clip from a popular movie, television program, or music video in *lectio divina* at a future meeting. Discuss with the group why you think this is a good idea. Be prepared for some mild resistance, especially among people with fixed ideas about prayer. There are some people, for example, who think *lectio divina* is only useful with biblical texts or inspirational poetry. Gently explain that this is an experiment and that you believe God can use all kinds of creative media for God's purposes.

In the film K-PAX, psychiatrist Mark Powell questions Prot (the character who says he's from a distant planet)

about his home. Prot tells him there are no laws on K-PAX, because K-PAXians do not need laws. Prot says, "Every being in the universe knows right from wrong, Mark."

That line has staying power for me. I wonder if I believe that. Does every being really know right from wrong? Or can we get to a point where we can no longer distinguish between the two?

I take that line, which seems to have meaning for me, into prayer to see what God is inviting me to notice.

I begin by repeating "every being in the universe knows right from wrong" silently to myself. This leads me to think about times when I have seemed to have a knowing of right from wrong. I think about how God granted me the gift of conscience and the freedom to use it or not. This prompts me to think of freedom and how much God must love us and trust us to give us these gifts. I rest in silence with God in that freedom. When I finish this prayer, I reach for my journal to write about the twin gifts of freedom and conscience.

—Teresa

Using *Lectio Divina* with Music

1. Decide what piece of music you want to pray with. You may want to use a musical piece that evokes some emotion in you.

2. As you listen, be aware of any image, word, phrase, or emotion that is called forth in you. When you settle on one, sit silently with it and bring your attention back to it when your attention strays. Allow the image, word, phrase, or emotion to deepen in you.

3. What does this image, word, phrase, or emotion have to say about your spiritual journey? How is it

related to your life? Ask God to reveal that to you.

4. Rest silently with your image, word, phrase, or emotion. Offer it to God. Wait patiently on God.

5. What would you like to express to God about the experience of praying with this piece of music? You may want to journal about it, share it with someone, or return to it in prayer at another time.

6. Thank God for whatever you received in this time of prayer.

In time, after you have practiced this method of prayer, you will want to use *lectio divina* on just about any experience in life. You can reflect upon any moment in your day that stands out and seems to have spiritual significance. You may even want to journal about your *lectio* experiences.

It is important to note that people may sometimes have a hard time finding images, words, phrases, or emotions that seem to draw them to a deeper relationship with God. That difficulty is perfectly normal. Prayer is openness to God, not the result of successful performance. Do not be discouraged if you or someone in your prayer group cannot get past step one of the *lectio* process. The more you stay open to the idea of God communicating through visual media, and the more you attempt this prayer practice, the more likely you will be to experience its benefits.

Using Luther's Four-Stranded Garland with Media

1. As before, choose the clip you want to pray with. Keep it short.

2. Ask God to be present in this prayer practice. Begin with a few moments of silence.

3. Play the chosen clip at least two times. Watch and listen for something in it—an image, word, phrase, or emotion—that seems to have a lesson for you. If you are alone, write down what you think this lesson may be. If in a group, each person may say aloud the insight he or she received.

4. Play the media clip again. Watch and listen for something in it that brings out a sense of gratitude and thanksgiving in you. Share that with the group, or make a note of it if you are alone.

5. Play the clip again. Watch and listen for something in it that draws you to confess a sin, shortcoming, or other spiritual block that stands between you and a healthy relationship with God. If you are alone, you may write down your confession. If in a group, be aware that some people may not feel comfortable sharing this part with the group. If you are the group leader, make sure it is clear that participants should only share what they feel safe sharing.

6. Play the clip once again. See if something in it feels like guidance in your life. Contemplate how God is present in the image, word, phrase, or emotion, and how God may be leading you. Share or write down your thoughts about guidance.

7. Close with a spoken or silent prayer, thanking God for being alive and present in the clip.

Using *Lectio Divina* with Children

Choose a media clip that is created for the age and development level of the child or children's group you are working with. Instead of isolating a small portion (as above), you may

want to watch a show that is known to be a children's favorite, and then follow this method.

1. Ask God to be present in the viewing, listening, or experiencing of the media clip. Trust God to be active in the life of the child or group as you experience this media clip. You may do this silently or spend a short time in spoken prayer. There is no particular need to explain that you are going to do a special prayer practice with the media.

2. Watch the progrĭam or clip together.

3. Ask the young viewers, "What is it about this show that you like best?"

4. If it is a short clip, watch it again. If it is a long program, go back to a portion of the show that seemed significant to the child or group you are with. Watch that portion again.

5. Again ask, "What was the best part of the show?" The idea is to get them to say more about the specific image or sound to which they are drawn.

6. Ask, "Is this like your life?" If yes, "How is it like your life?" If no, "How is it different from your life?"

7. Ask the child or children: "Is this the way God would have us live?" Draw them into a conversation about what they believe God wants for us.

8. Thank God for the time spent in prayer. Trust that God is present and at work in all aspects of childhood life.

Conclusion

God is revealed in all aspects of our ordinary life. Learning to allow a word, image, or sound to resonate deep within you and touch the core of your being is a time-tested way of being with God. It helps us notice that, as Prot declares, "Our planet is really bright." It allows that awareness to bring us into deeper relationship with the Light.

In the next chapter, the awareness found in *lectio* provides the foundation for a popular prayer exercise known as the Ignatian *examen*.

Notes

1. *The Rule of Saint Benedict*, ed. Timothy Fry, O.S.B. (New York: Vintage Books, 1981), 47.
2. Kathleen Norris, *The Cloister Walk* (New York: Riverhead Books, 1996), 31-46.
3. Martin Luther, *A Simple Way to Pray* (vol. 43 of *Luther's Works*; ed. Gustav K. Wiencke; trans. Carl J. Schindler, (Philadelphia: Fortress Press, 1968), 187-211.
4. Joseph D. Driskill, *Protestant Spiritual Exercises: Theology, History and Practice* (Harrisburg, Pa.: Morehouse Publishing, 1999), 93.

Chapter 2
Using the Ignatian *Examen* with Media

You know for an educated person, Mark,
you repeat things quite a bit.
Are you aware of that?
                    —*Prot to Dr. Powell*

Similar to *lectio divina*, the Ignatian prayer of *examen*, sometimes called the "Awareness Prayer," is an active prayer in which we examine something concrete in our life (our day, an event, or, in this case, a movie or television show) and ask how God reaches out to us in that space of time. In *lectio*, we searched for an image, word, phrase, or emotion that seemed significant to us. In the *examen* we do this as well, with one significant difference: We will consider both that which draws us closer to God and that which draws our attention away from God.

We do this by asking two important questions after viewing a clip, television episode, or feature film:

- In what moment during the story did I feel the most gratitude?

- In what moment during the story did I feel the least gratitude?

Although there are many different ways to word these questions to get to the heart of the matter, it is a good idea to begin with gratitude because most people, regardless of their reli-

gious tradition or background, understand the feeling of gratitude. It is also where the author of the *examen* prayer begins.

Ignatius of Loyola: Promoter of the *Examen*

Ignatius of Loyola, injured as a soldier in the battle of Pamplona in 1521, was left to convalesce in a home that contained books only about the life of Christ or of the saints. Being a man fond of romance novels (and not particularly religious at the time), Ignatius did a lot of daydreaming in bed. He also read books about Christ and the saints.

He began to notice how he felt after daydreaming about the chivalrous life versus daydreaming about living the simple life of a Christian saint. He noticed that he felt full of joy, love, and compassion when he visualized himself as a follower of Christ. He began to desire the life of a saint. Working primarily from this desire, Ignatius followed his heart and became the founder of the Jesuit Order.

One of Ignatius' great contributions to spirituality is his advice to Christians to "ask for what we desire" at the beginning of every prayer session.[1] What Ignatius refers to is our deepest and truest desires—the ones that please God and bring us into deeper relationship with God.

Usually done at night, the *examen* is simple and can be done in as little time as ten minutes.

1. Begin by settling into prayer and asking God's love to envelope your being as you pray. Ask God to bring to mind the parts of the day that are most significant to you.

2. Think back over your day.

3. Ask yourself:
   a. In what moment did I feel the most gratitude?
   b. In what moment did I feel the least gratitude?

4. Let God reveal to you, in those moments, God's love and invitation to you.

5. End by thanking God for what you have learned.

Many people who practice the daily *examen* make notes in their personal journals about high and low moments. Over time, they notice how actions and their resulting feelings repeat themselves. This is how we begin to see our own life patterns and the unique way God works in our lives.

Ignatius named the moments of most gratitude *consolation*, and the moments of least gratitude *desolation*; and he urged people to chart and notice those parts of life that brought on the two movements.

Consolation is generally where we are moving toward God, and desolation is generally where we are moving away from God. That does not mean that we have to feel joyful all of the time that we are moving toward God; it is more complex than that. But at our core, when we are following God's lead, we are generally at peace and we experience love. When we are anxious, fearful, and cut-off from God, we are usually somehow "off the path."

You do not have to understand everything there is to know about consolation and desolation to do the *examen*. Try the daily *examen* for at least a month and see if you begin to find patterns of how God is revealing God's self to you. For more detailed information about the *examen* and some of its variations, see the book *Sleeping with Bread* by Dennis Linn, Sheila Fabricant Linn, and Matthew Linn.[2]

Ignatian spirituality is rooted in an understanding of the movements of God's Holy Spirit in our deepest and truest feelings as we feel our way along the spiritual journey. The *examen* is the simplest way to begin to see God's hand at work in our life. It is also one of the simplest tools you can use with media and is especially good with children, provided the questions are kept simple.

Putting Visual Media to the *Examen*

Although the *examen* is fine to use for personal reflection, it can be very beneficial to use this spiritual practice in a group, perhaps after everyone experiences the same film, television episode, video, or even computer game.

The beauty of using the *examen* with a group after watching a film, television show, or video clip is that the group prays together while it also draws significant meaning from today's most popular stories. This can expose individuals to a prayer experience that they may not have known before. For example, for some members of youth groups, it may be that the film is the attractive element, but the prayer is what "sticks with them" for the future.

For the *examen* discipline to work most effectively, keep a written record of your responses to a variety of media over a long space of time, perhaps over a month or two. This will help you gauge how your life in the Spirit is being affected by your media consumption.

I don't believe in censorship, nor do I believe it is right for me to tell people what is "good" to watch and what is "bad." Each person has to discover that for himself or herself. But, it was the examen that showed me that violent

films are not healthy for me. As a result, I began to avoid them, and I feel better.

Before I started praying the examen, *I wanted to see all of the popular films that people were talking about. However, as I kept recording in my journal how I felt after watching violent films, I grew more and more uncomfortable with the feelings that were revealed. One particularly bloody torture scene in the film* Bound *left me feeling anxious, frightened, and unable to sleep one evening. I looked through my* examen *journal and saw that I frequently felt this way after watching violent TV shows or films. I saw that these feelings were affecting my spiritual journey and that, if I wanted to be healthy, I needed to give them up.*

Prior to using the examen, *if I had felt that God was asking me to give up popular films, I might have felt resentful and punished. The* examen *practice of prayer taught me about being in partnership with God. My feelings are important both to God and to me. I have to honor them. I was brought to a place where now I use my free will to say no. That's what I believe the* examen *can do for each of us—show us the way and gently encourage us to follow God's path.*

—Teresa

Because the *examen* asks each person to look into himself or herself for the movement of God's Spirit, it is ideal for use with young people, who tend to be wary of any adult who takes a "preachy" tone with them, especially around media. Make sure you keep the open-ended questions truly open. Do not judge people's responses. If you lead this prayer with a group, make sure no one presses his or her theology or ideology on anyone else, and stop that person if he or she does. We need to trust that God will reach each person where each is.

As I did the prayer of examen with K-PAX I began to notice that every time my mind rested on a scene of Prot interacting with the mental patients, I would feel a sense of peace and joy. However, as I remembered the scenes of the doctors discussing Prot, I often felt agitated and even angry. As my time of prayer deepened, what came to mind was a saying that I have often heard in church circles: "The purpose of the gospel is to comfort the afflicted and afflict the comfortable."

As Prot dealt lovingly with the mental patients, the afflicted, I felt the comfort and consolation of the message of Jesus. However, as the doctors (those with comfort and status in society) rejected Prot and his message, I felt the affliction of this same message. These observations helped me think about my own life and the times when I have been open to accepting God's message, and times when I have refused to notice God because somehow the gospel was challenging me in my sense of comfort and self-assurance.

—Daniel

Try It at Home or in a Group

1. Choose a film, television show, or salient video clip to watch. If taking it to a group, watch it beforehand to make sure it is appropriate for that group.

2. Begin the group meeting with a prayer, reminding everyone that they will be watching prayerfully. Give them the questions beforehand so they can watch for significant moments.

3. Watch the video story together.

4. At the end, give some silent time to allow the group to reflect on what members have seen and to think about the following questions (let them choose the ones that make sense to them).

5. In what moment did you feel the most gratitude?
   a. In what moment did you feel the most life? Love? Joy? Appreciation? Connected to God?
   b. What was the "high point" of the story for you?

And then,

6. In what moment did you feel the least gratitude?
   a. In what moment did you feel the most drained? Unloving? Anxious? Fearful? Disconnected from God?
   b. What was the "low point" of the story for you?

7. Go back to a time of silence and ask people to think about what gift God may have for them in the viewing of that story.

8. End with a prayer of thanksgiving for the blessing of the story, its makers, and God's revelations to us through it.

Conclusion

Many people find the *examen* to be an essential part of their Christian lives. Years after Ignatius had become the leader of the Jesuits, several members of his order came to him and complained that they did not have much time for prayer in the midst of their busy lives. Ignatius told them that they could set aside all prayers except the one that he felt was most

important: the daily *examen*. After practicing this discipline over a period of time, you may also find it important in your life. Doing the *examen* over a stretch of time (weeks, months, a year) provides a good foundation for the subject of our next chapter, the rich and intricate practice of spiritual discernment.

Notes

1. George E. Ganss, S.J., ed., *Ignatius of Loyola: The Spiritual Exercises and Selected Works* (New York: Paulist Press, 1991), 130.
2. Dennis Linn, Sheila Fabricant Linn, and Matthew Linn, *Sleeping with Bread: Holding What Gives You Life* (Mahwah: Paulist Press, 1995).

Chapter 3
Using Discernment with Media

If I can just prove him wrong, maybe I can find out who he really is.
—Dr. Mark Howell, talking to his brother-in-law about Prot

In the previous chapter, the prayer practice of the *examen* was used to look for "God moments." The *examen* allowed us to see glimpses of God's presence and absence within our experience of media. In this chapter, the search for God's presence will broaden by praying into entire stories using the practice of discernment.

Finding a deeper story within a story is the essence of discernment. The biblical writers all looked into the stories of their times and tried to find another story, the story of how God was working in their world. The Bible is the result of such a search for story, and successive generations have used these sacred texts as a springboard from which to search for meaning within the thousands of plots and subplots that bombard us every day.

The "soccer moms" were gathered around the table in the school kitchen, chatting about their kids' lives and cleaning up after serving a lunch of pizza to the children at school— yet another fund-raiser to help pay for things left out of the school budget. My wife was one of the women involved in the event, so I had dropped in hoping

for a free piece of pizza, since they almost always had leftovers. And for a while I joined in the conversation.

Soon, we were talking about the new Pokemon movie that was all the rage among the elementary school crowd. This movie was based on the TV show, which was based on the trading card game, which was based on the phenomenally successful Nintendo game from Japan.

The game creates a world of 151 fantasy creatures with names such as Snorilax, Beedril, and Richu. These creatures are captured by the humans in our world and then trained to fight one another. The battles never result in the death of the creatures, but only their eventual exhaustion, at which point they give up and return to their trainer, their human captor.

Already a worldwide hit, Pokemon had finally made its big-screen Hollywood début. Most of the mothers present that day had oldest children a few years younger than our children, so they had not yet been required to zoom over to the theater and see this latest cultural icon. However, some of their kids were pushing hard, and these parents wanted to know what they had to look forward to.

My wife and I told them about the film and answered all of the usual questions: How violent is it? How scary? and so on. Then I added that what was really interesting to me about the film was that the plot was really the same as the story of Jesus. The room got very quiet. One mother asked what I meant.

I told them that the whole movie was the story of the battle between good and evil, each represented by a particular Pokemon. At the end of the movie, as the battle is getting worse and worse, threatening to destroy all of the Pokemon, Ash, one of the human trainers, in an effort to stop the fighting, jumps between two of the battling Pokemon and is killed. This stops the fighting, and the

*resulting release of love resurrects Ash: The Poke-world is
saved by his sacrifice.*

*I finished my story, and my friend looked at me and
said, "That sends chills down my spine."*

—Daniel

In our time, story has once again become vitally important.
People are looking more to their own experience as a source
of truth, as objective norms and ideas are increasingly rejected. The result of this is that we are seeking meaning within
the stories of our lives. We are once again in an age in which
we are looking for God within story: our story, the story of
our community, the stories we see on the screens we gaze
into.

Because media is a primary conveyer of story, it is an ideal
subject for the prayer of discernment, a prayer that seeks to
find God in story. The woman in the school lunchroom felt
chills down her spine because suddenly she became aware
that a seemingly trivial children's film actually contained reference to a larger and far more profound story. Yet without
the ability to discern this larger pattern, she would have
missed the connection.

Why is discernment such an issue when it comes to God?
Well, very simply, because God is invisible. If God were a
clear, present person in our lives, then discernment would
not be necessary. We would speak to God directly and that
would be that. However, we are not so lucky. God is, as one
hymn puts it, "silent as light." In fact, God often appears to be
so absent that millions of people do not even believe in the
existence of God.

This seeming lack of presence requires that we discern God's
presence amid the thousands and thousands of events, perceptions, and bits of sensory data that bombard us every wak-

ing hour. This task is made even more difficult by the fact that no two people see these events and perceptions in exactly the same way. Discernment is not just an individual phenomenon; it is something that must be done in community.

It is not an exaggeration to say that the discernment of God's presence is perhaps the most important and central activity of a community of faith. Unfortunately, many individuals and faith communities shrink from this challenge. It is easier to exist in the illusion of false agreement in which all are silent about what they believe as they sit next to one another in church, pretending that they all know what the Trinity is really about.

When we enter into the process of discernment, we risk entering into chaos as we admit that perhaps we know nothing about God and God's presence. It is a tough challenge, but not unlike the one given to Abraham and Sarah, who set off into the desert in search of a land they did not know. It is the risk of Jesus in the garden crying out, "Take this cup from me." Discernment requires courage and practice.

Discernment also requires a guide, and this is one of the main functions of the Bible. The Church has always used Scripture as a series of examples, a series of stories, about how God is active and present in the lives of human beings. As we come to know these stories, we can begin to compare them to the stories that we see in our own lives. This helps us begin to notice the presence of the Divine. It can also help us notice just the opposite: when something is not of God.

This process of taking notice is at the heart of the spiritual life. As we apply the prayer of discernment to the media we watch, we can use our "screen time" to more fully understand the influences that shape our view of reality, as well as give ourselves a chance to seek God in everything that surrounds us.

My sons, Sam and Max, at the time ages ten and seven, and I were watching TV. There was a commercial break, and the first ad to come on was for a car. Unfortunately, the kids know most of the commercials by heart, and this one was familiar to them. Max said, "This commercial is so dumb." "Yes," responded Sam, "It says that if you buy this car your life will be perfect." What followed was a wonderful discussion about what does and doesn't make a person happy, and what is really of value in life. We were also able to discuss how commercials try to replace the things of lasting value with their products in an effort to get you to buy the products.

—Daniel

What Daniel's kids had been able to do, as they stared, mesmerized, at the screen, was see the story within the story. The surface story in the commercial was fairly simple: Guy buys car; guy gets everything he could want in life; guy is incredibly happy. The story beneath the story was similar but more generalized: Buy the car, and ultimate happiness is yours.

Our faith tells us that the only true and lasting happiness comes from God. Our faith in Jesus and Jesus' gracious actions toward us is the only rock on which we can rely. All else is sinking sand. The commercial attempts to undermine this story and replace it with another story. The commercial's story says that if we have their particular stuff, we will be happy and our lives will be perfect. This is the familiar story of idolatry. If we worship the idol of wealth and materialism, we will be saved. The Bible constantly counsels against this approach to salvation. By being able to see the deeper story in the commercial, it was possible to discern that the commercial was promoting something that is not of God, and it was also possible to engage in a discussion of what is of God.

The real point of all of this is not just to critique TV shows or movies or commercials. Ultimately, the value of discernment is beginning to see how God is working in your own life. The ability to discern the story in the media becomes practice for discerning the patterns in your own stories. This is how we use the Bible. The real point of reading about Jesus healing someone is not so much to rejoice over the healing of someone long gone, but to know that Jesus can heal us now.

How can we practice the prayer of discernment with visual media? For this section, our movie, *K-PAX*, will serve as an example. You can do this prayer practice with a whole movie, a TV show, or just a media clip. Let us begin with a summary of the process and then go through the practice using the movie *K-PAX*.

Discernment Process with Media

1. Begin by noting your intention to seek the presence of God in the story you are about to watch. Spend some time in silence, opening yourself to the presence of the Spirit.

2. Watch the movie. You may wish to watch it through once and then go back to certain places that have gotten your attention. Parts of this prayer practice may be done while you are watching the film, but you will want to do most of the practice after you have watched.

3. Begin the discernment prayer by asking questions about the story. What type of story is it? What are the major themes or plotlines?

4. Once you have outlined the story, ask yourself, "In what way or ways does this remind me of the bib-

lical story? Does the movie's story remind me of a favorite Bible passage or character?"

5. As you notice these connections to the biblical story, move deeper into the process of prayer. As you discern the presence of the biblical story on the screen in front of you, you can begin to ask yourself questions about the presence of God in your life.

6. While praying with these questions, a particular situation or issue may come to mind: a decision you are trying to make; a question you are trying to resolve. Perhaps the story you are praying into in some way speaks to that issue. In the silence of your prayer, listen for what God may be saying to you. Once you are done with your time of prayer, thank God for being with you in your prayer practice.

Discernment Process with *K-PAX*

1. Begin by noting your intention to seek the presence of God in the story you are about to watch. Spend some time in silence opening yourself to the presence of the Spirit.

2. Watch *K-PAX*. You may wish to watch it through once and then go back to certain places that have gotten your attention.

3. Begin the discernment prayer by asking questions about the story. What type of story is *K-PAX*? What are the major themes or plotlines? For example, you may notice that it is a story of an unusual person who arrives in a situation, making fantastic

claims about himself. He seems to have extraordinary powers and abilities and appears able to help those around him.

4. Once you have outlined the story, ask yourself in what way or ways *K-PAX* reminds you of the biblical story. Does the story you are watching remind you of a favorite Bible passage or character? After watching *K-PAX*, Daniel realized that Prot reminded him of Jesus. The plot of the movie also reminded him of the Jesus story.

5. As you notice these connections to the biblical story, you move deeper into the process of prayer. As you discern the presence of the biblical story on the screen in front of you, you can begin to ask yourself questions about the presence of God in your life. While watching *K-PAX*, you may wonder what it would really be like to meet Jesus. What experiences have you had that remind you of such an encounter? How is Jesus in fact present in your life?

6. As you ask these questions, a particular situation or issue may come to mind, such as a decision you are trying to make, or a question you are trying to resolve. Perhaps the story you are praying into in some way speaks to that issue. In the silence of your prayer, listen for what God may be saying to you. Looking at *K-PAX*, you may be reminded of a relationship in which you feel the need to behave in a more Christ-like manner. Through doing the prayer of discernment with *K-PAX*, maybe God will speak to you about how this desire may be fulfilled. You can see more clearly how it is that Jesus may act in your situation.

7. Once you are done with your time of prayer, thank God for being with you in your prayer practice.

Conclusion

The process of discernment involves sifting through the layers and complexities of our lives so that we may arrive at the truth that is Jesus in our midst. It takes practice and requires that we focus our awareness on the stories around us. The media, especially TV and the movies, constantly present stories for our consumption. Some of these stories are similar to those of our faith, and some of them are stories that contradict the stories of Scripture.

Bringing our awareness to these stories can help us see them for what they are. It can also help us become more attuned to the stories in our lives. As we do this, we begin to see the work of the Divine shining all around us.

Chapter 4
Using Imaginative Prayer with Media

Let's jump right in, shall we?
—Scientist at observatory

Make sure you can swim
—Prot

We are blessed with active and creative imaginations, and we need to celebrate this gift. Stories presented as "virtual reality" are creative gifts and useful tools for exercising our imaginations. In turn, our imaginations are useful in prayer.

Letting our imaginations go in prayer may seem odd or some-what sacrilegious to some people. Are we not supposed to corral our thoughts and images and focus instead on God? Well, yes and no. As the writer of Ecclesiastes points out, "For everything there is a season" (Eccl 3:1). There is a time to use our imaginations and a time to give them a rest. This chapter focuses on an active imagination. A later chapter helps us rest our thoughts and images through apophatic or image-less prayer.

A prayer of the imagination is usually directed by either Scripture, written story, or, as is employed here, visual story. Have you ever watched a movie or TV show and later day-dreamed how you wished it had ended, or inserted scenes that you thought probably belonged in the story? That is active imagination.

If you have ever watched a film or TV show and later imagined yourself somehow in the storyline, reacting and taking initiative to change the outcome, then you know how to do this prayer! We will begin with the traditional prayers of Augustine and Ignatius, who used Scripture, and then move into a discussion of ways to share our media-inspired daydreams with God. Then we will call upon God to transform our daydreams into awareness of our self and our world.

At least two major figures in Christian history, Augustine and Ignatius of Loyola, understood the power of the imagination. Augustinian prayer has us take the situations found in Scripture and use our imagination to create situations that speak the same truth to us today.[1] This is identical to what many filmmakers and television producers do every day. They take themes from literature, including sacred Scripture, and present them in stories that retell old stories in new ways.

Ignatius urged those who underwent his retreat of spiritual exercises to allow the stories in Scripture to prod their imaginations, letting the biblical stories take on new life and direction in the heart of the retreatant.[2] Psychologist Carl Jung called this sort of practice "active imagination." It is intentional and prayerful daydreaming. In this chapter we will explore imaginative prayer in general and suggest ways to use it with visual stories found in the media.

To grasp the basics, we begin with an exercise that imaginatively inserts us into a story from the Gospel of Mark. It is a story that illustrates Jesus' popularity as a healer. Using your favorite translation, read Mark 2:1-12, the story of Jesus healing the paralyzed man.

Using Ignatian Imaginative Prayer with Scripture

1. Begin by becoming inwardly silent and open to the presence of God.

2. Read the passage slowly, pausing as the scene changes. As you pause, let your imagination run free. Where do you see yourself in the story? Which character would you most want to be? Which character are you drawn to? Where are you standing or sitting? What does the scene look like? Feel like? Smell like? Sound like?

3. Read the passage again, and continue to insert yourself into the story.

4. Sit silently, and imagine the scene expanding. What is your role?

5. If you are a person in the crowd, approach Jesus and have a conversation. If you like, write down what you and Jesus say to each other.

6. Imagine what may happen after the final scene ends. Where do you go? Where does Jesus go? What are the people saying in addition to what is written in the scripture?

7. Take some time to think about how God may have spoken to you in the midst of this imaginative prayer.

8. Finally, allow the scene to settle down and fade out.

9. Give thanks to God for Scripture, your imagination, and the Spirit-inspired interaction between the two.

How easy or difficult that exercise is will depend a lot on your personality. Creative artists who think visually will have the easiest time of it. Their visualizations will take wings and fly! People whose imaginations are less active may find it frustrating to try to visualize a time that is in the distant past. If you are the kind of person who is not given to flights of fancy or daydreaming, do not despair. Not every prayer practice is for every person. It is worth a try now and then, if only to give your imagination a workout.

If you are a highly rational person, you may be bristling at this point. "Talking to imaginary characters? New Age nonsense!" you may say. However, imaginative dialoging with historical characters has been around a lot longer than New Age practitioners. It is simply a way to change your perspective and think in new directions.

In this endeavor, you are talking to and exploring within yourself. However, in the context of prayer, this conversation has a higher purpose—to be honest and open in the presence of God. God will reveal to you what God needs you to know in the course of this prayer practice, even if you feel silly talking to a "teacher of the Law" or a disciple in your imagination.

Using Augustine's Imaginative Prayer with Scripture

1. Become quiet and attentive to God's presence.

2. Read the scripture twice.

3. Imagine how that scene would look or seem today, in our world.

4. How might you rewrite the story so that its message appeals to viewers or listeners today?

Using Imaginative Prayer with Visual Texts

Let us now turn our attention to visual texts, specifically to our feature film, *K-PAX*. How we might use this prayer practice with it? What is the difference between simply letting our minds drift and play with scenes from the movie and doing so in prayer? The difference is intention. Begin by asking God to speak to you in some way through your imagination.

After doing that, you could imaginatively place yourself in the setting of the film, perhaps as one of Prot's colleagues in the psychiatric hospital. Or you could see yourself as the therapist, or as an outsider who happens to meet Prot on the street. The character you choose to be is the one who seems most attractive to you. Who would you want to be in this film? Who might you want to get to know more? Who intrigues you the most? That is who you choose to have a dialog with or imagine that you accompany in a scene.

People who enjoy writing in journals will definitely want to do this type of imaginary dialog on paper. Others may want to let their minds soar unfettered by writing implements. Do what seems best to you.

If you feel your prayers and imaginings are going too far astray, you can always imagine Jesus entering the picture and returning the focus to him. However, do this out of need to center your thoughts, and not just because you feel you must do so in order to be a good Christian. God's Spirit can and will work through your imagination, whether you ritualistically invoke the name of Jesus or not.

Perhaps the ending of *K-PAX* seems ambiguous to you, as it does to many people. You may want to explore what really happened to Prot using the Augustinian method of imaginative prayer. Where did Prot go? Were he and Porter the same

person? How does the healing that he mentioned all humans having the capability to use, work?

One thing is sure: You will not know the value of this prayer practice for you unless you encounter it. If you have not practiced imaginative prayer with Scripture yet, do it now, using a vivid biblical story that means a lot to you. Then, try it with a film or television episode that moved you in some way in the past.

A Guide to the Ignatian Imaginative Prayer Practice with Media

1. Begin by becoming still and present to your own body. Gently draw your awareness first to your environment and then to the mysterious presence of God.

2. Ask God to speak to you through the visual media and your imagination. Also ask God to help you listen to what God may be saying in those images and scenes.

3. Watch the video. If you know the special scene you want to reflect on, isolate it. If you are watching an entire film or television episode on tape, then you may want to stop the tape at various intervals for some silence as you and others that may be with you take it in.

4. At the end of the clip or showing, determine how you feel most comfortable about imagining:
   a. Which scene do you want to explore?
   b. Out of which character's eyes do you want to see the scene?
   c. Do you want to be one of the characters or be in a crowd, observing?

5. After you decide on an insertion point and a point of view, let your imagination soar. Allow plenty of silence for this time. You may want to write out the scene; or, if you have the materials handy, you may paint, draw, or sculpt a representation.

6. Talk with one of the main characters about faith. Ask a question and see what he or she says.

7. If you so desire, invite Jesus into the scene. What happens then? Where does your conversation with Jesus go?

8. After a good deal of time has passed (fifteen minutes or so), imagine the scene coming to an end. Say goodbye to everyone. Express your gratitude for the guidance they gave you.

9. End by thanking God for the time together, and for your imagination and the gift of active imaginations.

This is a particularly good exercise to use with young people after watching a popular film together. If you do it with a group, provide paper, pens, and art supplies for creative expression, and allow the individuals to move about silently if they need to do so. That will make the fifteen minutes of silence seem less oppressive to those who have trouble sitting still. At the end of the silent time, ask participants who are willing to share their imaginative exploits in prayer. Keep an open mind about what they experience.

A Guide to Augustinian Imaginative Prayer Practice with Media

1. Begin by becoming still and present to your own body. Gently draw your awareness to your environ-

ment, and then become aware of the mysterious presence of God.

2. Ask God to speak to you through the visual media and your imagination. Also ask God to help you listen to what God may be saying through those images and scenes.

3. Watch the video. Determine at what point you would like to "rewrite" the story.

4. Let your imagination soar. Allow plenty of silence for this time. You may want to write out the new scene; or if you have the materials handy, you may want to paint, draw, or sculpt a representation.

5. Talk with one of the main characters about faith. Ask a question and see what he or she says.

6. If you so desire, invite Jesus into the scene. What happens then? Where does your conversation with Jesus go?

7. After a good deal of time has passed (fifteen minutes or so), imagine the scene ending. Say goodbye to everyone. Express your gratitude for the guidance given you.

8. End by thanking God for the time together, for your imagination, and for the gift of active imaginations.

I'm a big fan of happy-ending romances. When films and television shows have ambiguous endings, I like to imagine how reconciliation might happen.

In the May 2003 season finale of the CBS-TV drama Without a Trace, *the hero of the show, FBI Supervising Agent Jack Malone, spent a harrowing day securing the*

release of Agent Samantha Spade from a distraught hostage-taker. Malone convinced the gunman to allow an exchange—himself for Spade, who was suffering a bullet wound. This was more than a supervisor exchanging his life for the life of a subordinate. Malone, a married father of two, and Spade had been lovers. They had recently acknowledged that their affair was finally over.

Throughout the first season, viewers knew Malone was estranged from his wife and had picked up hints that he and Spade were involved with each other. However, little background information on Malone's marriage was ever revealed. All we knew was that it was broken.

During a long conversation between Malone and the hostage-taker (who was still deeply depressed over the loss of his wife in the World Trade Center terrorist attack two years before), Malone tells his captor about the mess his life has become. When the event ends peacefully, the show concludes with Malone going back home to his wife and two daughters. The final scene shows him sitting by the bedside of his sleeping wife, in tears.

In my prayerful imagination, I spin out the rest of the story. Malone's wife, deeply hurt by the extramarital affair, wakes up and sees that her husband is no longer estranged. After what has been one of the worst days of his life, he has returned, like the prodigal son, to the place where he knows he will be accepted with open arms. A conversation that the two should have had months ago takes place, and the reconciliation begins.

I spend some time in prayer and remembering what repentance and reconciliation feels like, deep in my bones. Reflecting on how generous God and my loved ones have been to me over the years, I rest in the Spirit, and I know that I am enough, just as I am now. Just as Malone brought his brokenness back home that night, I accept my own brokenness and bring it home to God this day. —Teresa

Conclusion

It is helpful to remember that, although we are inspired and held by God in our time of prayer, everything that we imagine is not a direct message or revelation from God. Nor are our imaginings demonic, even if they veer into the darkness. We need to hold all of our imaginings lightly, accepting that we are human and flawed, and so is our mind's eye. At the same time, useful information and inspiration can come from imaginative prayers.

Most of the spiritual disciplines discussed so far have been mystical, heart-oriented practices. In the next chapter, our attention turns to the rational, critical thinking skills that also are part of a prayerful reflection.

Notes

1. Chester P. Michael and Marie C. Norrisey, *Prayer and Temperament: Different Prayer Forms for Different Personality Types* (Charlottesville, Va.: The Open Door, 1991), 58.
2. George E. Ganss, S.J., ed., *Ignatius of Loyola: The Spiritual Exercises and Selected Works* (New York: Paulist Press, 1991).

Chapter 5
Using the Spiritual Discipline of Study with Media

Mark, Mark, Mark.
You haven't heard a thing I've said to you.
—*Prot to Dr. Powell*

The Christian spiritual discipline of study is an active form of prayer. We study because, to paraphrase the great Christian philosopher Irenaeus, "The mind fully alive glorifies God." This chapter discusses how principles of analysis and theological reflection assist in bringing our minds alive. Examples are given of how a visual text may be analyzed, and a variety of worksheets and methods are supplied. This information is designed to assist you in the simple and then more complex analyses and theological reflection on media.

The discipline of study has been considered throughout history as being more mind-oriented than heart-oriented. In reality, there is no head-heart split—all of what we are is embodied, and we use both mind and emotion in partnership all of the time.

Ministers and academics are well acquainted with the discipline of study. It is the loving devotion of sifting through information to find meaning, connection, and new ways of seeing. Much of the criteria applied to biblical, literary, and theological studies can easily be applied to visual media.

For example, think of the Hebrew book of Esther. One of this book's famous traits is that it does not once mention the name of God. Yet, it found a place in the sacred canons

for both Jews and Christians. The fact that it is focused wholeheartedly on the human struggle, rather than on divine grace, did not prevent readers from finding deep, God-centered connections in the text. If biblical scholars and theologians can work with the book of Esther, then we certainly can work with visual media that neither mention God nor seem, at first glance, to be God-centered.

To assist you in the theological analysis of media, principles of biblical exegesis are combined with principles used in the media literacy movement. Media literacy is informed awareness, defined by the Alliance for a Media Literate America (AMLA) as "the ability to access, analyze, evaluate and communicate information in a variety of forms—both print and non-print."[1] It is critical thinking applied to popular culture. It does not end with simply weighing the pros and cons of any particular media offering, but it promotes appropriate action based on that assessment. In fact, this spiritual discipline is a source of empowerment in our media-saturated culture. It helps bridge what some people feel is a gap between contemplation and action.

Kate Lewis, an Episcopal seminarian taking the media literacy class entitled "Television Through the Lens of Faith" at San Francisco Theological Seminary in the spring of 2002, is standing in front of a large screen, presenting her analysis of a thirty-seven-second news story on CNN Headline News. The video we see is narrated by a breathless anchorperson commenting on "the Church of the Nativity being turned into a makeshift hospital."

Here is the problem: The image we are looking at is not the Church of the Nativity. Although many viewers of CNN and many in our class have not been to Bethlehem, Kate Lewis has. She tells us the church shown in the video is instead the

*Church of All Nations on the Mount of Olives—a more pho-
togenic church quite a distance from the city of Bethlehem.*

*As the announcer talks about nuns giving medical care
to Palestinians in the Church of the Nativity, dubbed "the
birthplace of Jesus," we are watching monks at the Church
of All Nations standing over an altar. The results are not
only confusing, but also misleading. The class moves into
a long discussion about how trustworthy the images we see
in newscasts really are. We learned so much from this thirty-seven-second clip of CNN from one student who carefully analyzed it—much more than CNN would ever
teach us.*

—Teresa

How to Do Theological Reflection on Media

There are as many ways to reflect theologically on media as
there are people doing the reflecting. We have included a few
of our favorite methods. Listed below are the ten most important questions to ask when watching film or television.

1. Who created this story? Who owns the produc-
   tion company responsible for it?

2. Who is the audience for this story?
   How can you tell?

3. Whose point of view is favored? Whose is
   disfavored?

4. Where is the tension in this story? How is the tension relieved?

5. What are the dominant messages? What latent
   messages can you identify?

6. Why do you think people are watching this?

7. What is being sold as the solution (salvation) here?

8. How are the poor and oppressed depicted? Who is the "other" here?

9. Does this view of the world agree with yours, or clash with it?

10. After viewing this, is there a call to action for concerned citizens?

These are a few questions to get you thinking about how media are constructed. These examples have been culled from a variety of sources, and you may do the same, constantly honing and refining your own method of theological analysis of media.

A shorter set of questions comes from a seminary class on interpreting the four Gospels.[2] We simply substituted the phrase "watch the media piece" for the professor's phrase "read the text."

1. Watch the media piece. If it is short, such as a news story or commercial, watch it several times.

2. Ask yourself:
   a. What assumptions do we bring to this story?
   b. Who is telling this story? Who is the author? What is that person's point of view?
   c. What is the storyteller saying to us? Why?
   d. How does the story challenge us?

The first analysis is performed on a commercial that spent many months in heavy play after debuting during the 2003 Super Bowl, featuring the Osbourne family for soft drink Pepsi Twist.

The ad begins with the father, rock star Ozzy Osbourne, trying unsuccessfully to attach a garbage bag to his trash drawer. He is mumbling and fumbling when his two children, Jack and Kelly, come up to him and show him their Pepsi cans. "These are not Pepsis," says Jack. "They're Pepsi Twists!" and they zip off the can covers to reveal the "twist." "And," says Kelly, "we're not the Osbournes. We're [they zip off their body covers] the Osmonds!" Donny and Marie Osmond appear and start to sing their old hit "I'm a Little Bit Country."

Daddy Osbourne wakes from his nightmare and screams for his wife, Sharon. He turns to her and instead sees Florence Henderson, who starred as the mother in the television series *The Brady Bunch* in the 1970s. The ad ends with the Osbourne kids mugging for the camera with lemon slices over their teeth, and a logo of Pepsi Twist. A voiceover says, "It's the Twist."

◆ What assumptions do we bring to this story?

First, the producers assume that we know the Osbournes from their weekly MTV sitcom. We who watch the show assume that whatever the Osbournes do will be ridiculous, profane, and entertaining. Viewers have seen Ozzy fuss with garbage bags before. We have seen the kids gang up on Dad. We also assume that the Osbournes are popular and the Osmonds are passé. The Osbourne kids are dressed in fashionable, street-style, casual clothes, while the Osmonds are in brightly colored, out-of-date costumes. We assume that the Osbournes are very different from the Osmonds and the Brady Bunch, especially since many of us have read media reports about the Osbournes that frequently point out that "they're not the Brady Bunch."

◆ Who is telling this story?
◆ Who is the author?
◆ What is that person's point of view?[3]

Since the piece is a commercial, Pepsi-Cola is the ultimate storyteller. Omnicom Group's BBDO Worldwide, led by chief creative officer Ted Sann, created the ad.[4] BBDO is famous for creating memorable Super Bowl advertisements. In 2002, it dominated Super Bowl commercial airtime with the Britney Spears "Now and Then" series of ads featuring the pop star performing in a variety of eras. The company has a reputation for creating ads that connect emotionally with the consumer.[5]

◆ What is the storyteller saying to us, and why?

The storyteller here is saying that things are not as they seem with Pepsi Twist. This cola, not well known at this point in time, may be misunderstood. We need to try it to find out what the "twist" is all about. The story also persuades us that popular people such as the Osbournes are drinking Pepsi Twist. The hope is that we will want to mimic the popular people. If we have positive associations with the Osbournes, we may begin to have positive associations with the soft drink as well.

◆ How does the story challenge us?

It goads us into chuckling about Ozzy's wacky home life, and it challenges us to remember pop culture icons from the 1970s. Its goal is to get us to purchase a new soda, which will put us in the valuable (to the advertisers and broadcasters) position of consumer.

The Meland Method

Another effective and more involved method for the theological analysis of media is inspired by the theology of Bernard Meland, a mid-twentieth-century scholar with a keen openness to the idea of God approaching us through culture.[6] Meland begins his theology with the human experience of God, which makes it appropriate for our use since almost all media explores the human experience rather than taking the viewpoint of the Divine.

Meland developed a four-step system for moving from the concrete experience of culture to our faith experience of God.

◆ Step One: Become Aware of the Text

"Appreciative awareness" is a term Meland use to express receptivity to the idea of God being revealed to us in culture. For some, that is a well-understood awareness. For others, it is an idea that takes some getting used to.

We become aware of the text by asking the questions: "What makes this visual text important to me? Why am I taking a closer look?"

◆ Step Two: Identify with the Text

Similar to appreciative awareness, identification asks you to be pulled into the event in a more intuitive and empathetic way. For this step, ask the question: "What do I notice about the film that resonates deeply within me?"

◆ Step Three: Analyze the Story

This is where you consider the narrative and ask yourself the following questions:

1. What is the tension in this story? How is it relieved?

2. What are the dominant messages? What background messages can I identify?

3. Why do I think people are watching this?

4. What is being sold as the solution (salvation) here?

◆ Step Four: Allow Our Faith Experience to Interact with the Text

This step brings us to the heart of the matter. Here is where we integrate our faith experiences with what we are watching. As we begin to make the connections, we will see even more connections. Some people will go to this step intuitively and naturally.

In this step we ask the following questions:

1. Is the image of God portrayed here one that I recognize or have experienced?

2. Does the spiritual dilemma here ring true for me? Why or why not?

3. Does the solution (salvation) seem healthy?

4. How does this story resonate with my life and my spiritual journey?

Here is the Meland Method outlined in the four steps with key questions:

◆ Step One: Become Aware of the Text

What makes this visual text important to me? Why do I want to take a closer look?

◆ **Step Two:** Identify with the Text

What do I notice about the text that resonates deeply within me?

◆ **Step Three:** Analyze the Story

1. What is the tension in this story? How is it relieved?

2. What are the dominant messages? What background messages can I identify?

3. Why do I think people are watching this?

4. What is being sold as the solution (salvation) here?

◆ **Step Four:** Allow Our Faith Experience to Interact with the Text

1. Is the image of God portrayed here one that I recognize or have experienced?

2. Does the spiritual dilemma portrayed here ring true for me? Why or why not?

3. Does the salvation (solution) seem healthy?

4. How does this story resonate with my life and spiritual journey?

Using the Meland Method with *K-PAX*

Now we will apply these questions to our feature film, *K-PAX*. Keep in mind that the way we, the authors, answer the questions will simply reflect what it seems to be saying to us. Your answers will probably be quite different. A healthy discussion of the differences can be enlightening, especially in a small group.

◆ Step One: Become Aware of the Text

What makes this visual text important to us? Why do we want to take a closer look?

It is important because of the way it makes us think about how we might treat someone such as Prot, who is vastly different from us and who has incredible gifts. Do we embrace him, as the mental patients did? Or do we declare him mentally ill and dismiss him? Is there an in-between? It makes Christians in particular think about how we might treat Jesus if we were to meet him in mod-ern-day form, without the church teachings and history behind us. In some ways, the film can be considered an answer to the question: What is the experience of being with a nonviolent yet infinitely powerful and compas-sionate being?

◆ Step Two: Identify with the Text

What do we notice about the film that resonates deeply within us?

Prot has many characteristics of a divinely gifted person: he heals; he has an innate sense of right and wrong; he brings out the best in many of our forgotten citizens.

Prot is disdainful of many human characteristics: our penchant for violence; our lack of awareness about the beauty of our planet; our small-mindedness.

The psychiatrist is portrayed as a person struggling with his desire to learn from Prot and to learn about Prot. He is challenged to think beyond his usual parameters as a psychotherapist.

The movie makes us wonder if Prot is really from another planet, or if he is, in fact, a deeply disturbed human who somehow had a break with reality.

◆ **Step Three:** Analyze the Story

1. What is the tension in this story? And how is it relieved?

The tension is around whether to believe Prot is a disturbed human or a being from another planet. There are clues that point to both answers, and no definitive answer is provided. If he is not an alien from another planet, how do we explain all of the strange things happening through and around him?

The tension is not relieved in the film, which makes it ambiguous and open-ended. On the one hand, Prot appears to remain in the hospital after declaring that he was heading back to the planet K-PAX. That would indicate that he was more mental patient than alien. On the other hand, it is clear that the person remaining is not the same in spirit as Prot. The mental patients insist that Prot is gone. Are we to believe them, though? After all, they are mentally ill.

Prot's remaining institutionalized also creates the problem of accounting for the strange things he did and knew about.

2. What are the dominant messages? What background messages can we identify?

There are several strong messages here:
  - *We do not treat very well people who are differently gifted from us.*

- *If we were to be in touch with beings of higher intelligence, we would likely institutionalize them if we were able.*

- *We have not yet moved from a belief that doctors heal to a belief that holds that the power of healing resides within us.*

- *We are too limited in our thinking and need to be open to possibilities that cannot be explained by current science and technology.*

- *Those in power are just as lost and mentally ill as the patients.*

- *Aliens from other planets exist in a state of peace, sanity, and unity. We earthlings are the ones who are violent, insane, and prone to self-destruction.*

- *Those in power are inclined to believe what they already believe. They are not open to new interpretations of reality, because their worldview has worked for them, as proved by their success.*

- *Love heals all.*

3. Why do we think people are watching this?

In reality, not too many people saw this movie. The box office receipts were disappointing to the producers. It is possible that film audiences are not as interested in heroes who are not macho or violent. Prot doesn't behave like the typical film hero. He allows himself to be imprisoned, held captive, humiliated, and drugged and does nothing violent to right the injustices he suffers.

For those who did choose to watch the film, they probably chose it because of its mystical elements. Science fiction shows us what might be, and challenges us to openness. We like to consider possibilities that are outside of the realm of experienced reality.

4. What is being sold as the solution (salvation) here?

> • *Getting off the planet!*
>
> • *Opening our minds to possibilities outside the realm of experienced reality.*
>
> • *Mysticism.*
>
> • *The power of love.*

◆ Step Four: Allow Our Faith Experience to Interact with the Text

1. Is the image of God portrayed here one that we recognize or have experienced?

   • *Certainly. Prot is a character fashioned in the image of Jesus. He is powerful and peaceful. He refuses to resort to violence when he is treated unjustly.*

2. Does the spiritual dilemma portrayed here ring true for us? Why or why not?

   • *The dilemma—how to respond with grace and love when treated unjustly—is one that is treated in many stories in the Bible. Its rendition in K-PAX rings true both in the human experience of many Christians and in the many stories of how God has worked throughout history with God's people.*

3. Does the salvation (solution) seem healthy?

   • *Salvation in this case is nonviolent love. That is not only healthy, but also in keeping with what Christians believe about Jesus' life, death, and resurrection.*

4. How does this story resonate with our lives and our spiritual journeys?

   • *The spiritual life is one of radical renunciation and radical empowerment. The bonds of the world no longer hold*

us, because we are freed through the power of the resurrected Jesus. As we live into this power, it doesn't matter where we find ourselves—in this case, a mental institution—because in everything we can see, experience, and bring to bear the love of God.

Conclusion

Take the time to do some in-depth theological analysis on a visual text. The time you spend in analysis will pay off in a deeper understanding of how the media messages are constructed and how they function in society.

Once you develop this kind of awareness, you will not look at visual media casually again. That does not mean you will not be able to relax and enjoy films and television. It simply means you will likely be changed from a passive viewer to an active participant.

From study we move to silence and centering. Virtual reality can be overwhelming, and just because we pray with it does not mean we need more of it in our lives. In the final chapter we will explore the necessity of imageless prayer in a world that is brimming with images.

Notes

1. A definition and description of media literacy can be found at the website of the Alliance for a Media Literate America (http://nmec.org/medialit.html). Accessed May 23, 2003.
2. We are grateful to Dr. Anne Wire, professor of New Testament at San Francisco Theological Seminary, for passing along this basic method.
3. For background information on writers, producers, and directors of all kinds of visual media, Internet searches are most helpful. For film, start with www.imdb.com. Television research generally begins with the network's main website for basic information, and then you will

need to search on the particular show or producer's name. Also, http://televisionwithoutpity.com/ is useful if the show you are interested in is included in its coverage. For commercials, begin with www.adcritic.com.

4. Information on this ad can be found on the following websites: www.superbowlads.com and www.pepsitwist.com/osbournes. Accessed May 29, 2003.

5. "Sann: From the Bronx to BBDO," March 30, 2001. Found online at www.bandt.com.au/articles/3e/0c002e3e.asp, the website of B & T Marketing and Media. Accessed May 29, 2003.

6. J. J. Mueller, *What Are They Saying about Theological Method?* (New York: Paulist Press, 1984).

Chapter 6
Using Imageless Prayer in an Image-Filled World

Even your Christ had quite a different vision,
but nobody's paid much attention to [him]
—not even the Christians.
—Prot

In the previous chapters, several different types of prayer with which to examine media have been presented. We have reflected on images, studied the content of commercials, examined our sense of gratitude, and discerned the presence of God, all using the content of the media as the starting point for the process of prayer. In this final chapter we take another approach. Here is presented a prayer practice that will help us experience the imageless God who lies behind, between, and around the media that we watch: the prayer of silent contemplation.

Jesus presented us with a different vision. He understood that "the Kingdom of God is among you" (Luke 17:21). God is everywhere, and we can access a spiritual space within which the law of Divine Love reigns supreme. However, this space is hard to inhabit. The paradox of turning to the media as a tool for prayer is that, whereas media can be a source of prayer and knowledge of God, it can also be a major distraction to our spiritual life.

When we are constantly bombarded with images, we can become a prisoner of these images and trapped within a commercial world of consumption. Our world can become a

place controlled by those who produce what we see on TV and in the movies. In the context of prayer with media, the purpose of silent contemplation is to create the space we need to see God operating both beyond and within the media we consume.

Silent Contemplation in the History of Our Faith

Silent contemplation, or silent prayer, has been with us for as long as our spiritual ancestors have been praying. The psalmist tells us to "be still and know that I am God!" (Ps 46:10). Even one of Abraham's servants "gazed . . . in silence to learn whether or not the LORD had made his journey successful" (Gen 24:21).

Once the church was established, praying in silence became one of the most important prayer practices for those who wished to "Let the same mind be in you that was in Christ Jesus" (Phil 2:4). In the third and fourth centuries, thousands of men and women went out into the desert to pray by themselves, some of them spending decades in the quiet of the hillside caves. When monastic communities began to form in the fourth and fifth centuries, the leaders of those communities prescribed several hours a day of silent prayer for their monks and nuns.

In the fourteenth century in England, an unknown author penned a book entitled *The Cloud of Unknowing*, which describes in detail the practice of silent prayer. This book has become a spiritual classic and is the basis for several modern versions of silent prayer, including centering prayer and Christian Meditation.[1]

What this prayer of silence takes very seriously is the notion that God is mystery; the Divine is beyond all that we can

think or know of God. Anything we say about God pales in comparison to the reality of the trinitarian persons. If this is true, then we who desire to know God must allow our minds to become empty of everything so that God can fill us with the "light of the world." The process by which this happens is silent prayer.

The Practice of Silent Contemplation

Unlike the other techniques in this book, silent prayer is not something to be done while watching a media clip. Rather, this is a prayer technique that will complement your media reflection and will help you with the other prayers presented in the book.

The actual technique of silent prayer is deceptively simple. Before you start your time of silence you will need to choose a word that you will use during your prayer time, a word that reminds you of your intention to know God. At the same time, it is important to realize that it does not really matter what word you pick. You cannot choose the "wrong" word. Some examples might be "God," "Jesus," "love," "peace," and so on.

1. Once you have chosen the word, decide on a period of time for silent prayer. Twenty minutes is a good amount of time with which to begin.

2. Find a comfortable place to sit. Make sure that your back is straight. Place your hands in a comfortable position on your lap. The prayer is most commonly done with eyes closed, but if this becomes uncomfortable, feel free to open them.

3. Begin by noting your intention to spend time with God.

4. Then sit in silence.

5. When you notice thoughts and other distractions coming to your mind, silently speak your word as a way of coming back to the silence. You should not be repeating your word over and over again, but rather use your word as a way of returning to your intention to be with God.

6. When your time is up, end your prayer with "Amen."

That is all! Now, although the technique is simple, the experience is often far from easy. You will encounter many distractions, thoughts, and feelings, including the sensation that you are doing it incorrectly. However, it is impossible to do this prayer incorrectly. Any time you notice that you are distracted in any way, simply return to your word.

The first few times you practice this prayer technique it may seem ridiculous. You may think, "I'm not getting it," or "I'm not getting anything out of it." However, this is not the point. In silent prayer, we are allowing God to get us. We are placing ourselves before our Maker in the posture of the dependant creature. We are allowing ourselves to be at God's disposal so that God may come and find us.

Through the technique of silent prayer, we are allowing ourselves to experience the space in which the Divine dwells. We begin to realize that our thoughts come and go, our feelings come and go, and none of them are God. Rather, we begin to realize that God may dwell in the space between our thoughts and feelings. This is what we mean when we say, "God speaks through our ideas or something we experience."

Silent Prayer in Groups

Because the practice of silent prayer is challenging, it is often good to attempt it in a group setting. It is done much the same way that you would do it in solitude.

1. Choose someone to lead the prayer. This person will be the timekeeper and will announce the beginning and the end of the prayer time.

2. Once everyone is seated comfortably, the leader begins the prayer by saying, "Let us pray."

3. After the twenty or thirty minutes are over, the leader says, "Amen." Another variation on these starting and ending techniques is to use some sort of bell or gong. Chimes are a traditional way for times of prayer to begin and end in Christian communities.

4. After the time of prayer, it can be helpful to have the group debrief the prayer experience. The focus here should be not on critiquing the prayer experiences, but on giving one another support to continue in the practice of silent prayer.

You will find that praying with others helps you stay faithful to the practice. Also, as you pray with others, you will begin to notice the fruits of the prayer. Most people experience a sense of love for the members of their prayer groups. The Holy Spirit moves among you in the silence, and the fruits of the Spirit begin to be revealed among the group's members.

Silent Prayer and Visual Media

I clearly remember the first time I watched K-PAX. I was a bit hesitant even to rent the movie, as I didn't want to watch another corny alien film. However, as I sat looking at the screen, I began to notice a thought welling up inside me. It was accompanied by one of those tingling sensations when all of the hairs on the back of your neck stand up. Finally the thought formed itself clearly in my mind, "I'm watching a movie about Jesus. Being with Prot—this is what it would be like to be with Jesus." The power of this realization was stunning, and it came to me out of the space and silence of my mind as I watched.

—Daniel

What does this silent prayer have to do with watching media? Remember, this is not a prayer practice that you do while you watch TV. It is not even one you use to analyze a movie or reflect back upon an experience of the media. So how are the two things, silence and media, connected?

We live in a world of images and media. Pictures come at us continuously from screens, magazines, even billboards, and store windows. In many ways, the constant presence of these images is much like the constant presence of our thoughts. When we sit in silence, we realize that our thoughts are also with us always, moving through our minds in a seemingly endless and solid stream. These thoughts and feelings define our internal reality as certainly as the images of the media increasingly define our external reality. If we never know what it is like to experience the space between our thoughts, then it is hard to recognize when God enters into our lives.

When we approach media in a prayerful manner, it is helpful if we have an experience of spiritual space. We learn to hold lightly anything we see on a screen through the practice of silent prayer. We are less likely to become so absorbed in the images we see that we are no longer open to the presence of God.

In the example above, I was able to hear something coming to me from beyond the movie. Even while I was watching the film, there was enough space in my experience for me to be open to another voice. The receptive posture of silent prayer allowed me to be receptive to God in the presence of media, just as I am receptive to God in the presence of my thoughts as I do the prayer practice.

Another way of stating the connection between silent prayer and prayer with media is that silent contemplation strengthens our intention.

With each of the prayer practices discussed so far, it is important to begin the prayer time by bringing to consciousness your intention to notice God through your media experience. Silent prayer increases our awareness of this desire to be in God's presence. It becomes easier to remember that we are seeking God in all that we do and all that we are. We no longer view media for its own sake, but focus more on the question of how God is speaking to us through our experience. Silent prayer helps us remain open to the unknown in our experience.

Once at a conference, I had lunch with several youth ministers. During the meal, one of them began describing how he was going to use The Matrix *with his youth group. He was quite excited about his plans and talked all about the numerous insights he had gotten about the gospel from*

the movie. After he finished describing his plans, one of the older members of our group said, "You need to remember that while you are having all of these postmodern insights, the average thirteen-year-old boy is just seeing a lot of people shooting one another."

This comment revealed to me the power of the media to distract us as well as enlighten us.

—Daniel

If we do not cultivate the practice of silence, we run the risk of being much like the thirteen-year-old boys watching *The Matrix*. The author of *The Cloud of Unknowing* tells readers that God exists within a cloud that our normal thoughts can not penetrate.

God is mystery, and it is only through silent prayer that we are able to move into the cloud and allow God to know us. The more we practice silent contemplation, the more all of the other prayers in this book will bear fruit. We will be able to listen for God more clearly in *lectio divina*. We will be able to experience our consolations and desolations through the *examen*. Our discernments will become more accurate. Our imaginative prayers will be more vivid, and our study will have greater focus and bear more fruit. As silence becomes part of our being, God will be able to speak to us out of the midst of even the most complex series of images.

Conclusion

There is an old saying that "the more things change, the more they remain the same." In the early years of the church, well into the sixteenth and seventeenth centuries, most Christians were illiterate. The message of the gospel came to them either by their listening to the written word, or through images.

This is why ancient cathedrals were so full of images, not because the people were idolatrous, but because the statues, paintings, and stained glass helped tell the biblical stories to peasants who could not read. These artistic renditions brought the Word of God to life and helped people hear the good news.

Now, most people in America can read, but interestingly, we are returning to a time rich with images. More and more people embrace images as their primary way of receiving information and understanding the world around them. This is just as true in religious life as it is in the secular arena.

Thus, as society "changes and remains the same," we believe it is vitally important for the health of the institutional church that it embrace and promote a greater variety of prayer practices, especially those that incorporate images. We have included a few of the oldest and most beloved prayer practices of Christianity in this book in the hope that as churches move toward a more visual approach in worship, they will also become equipped to teach and use more than the familiar prayers of intercession, petition, and a few of seconds of silence, especially in worship.

If you have attempted the prayer practices in this book, you are probably amazed at how simple and meaningful the practices can be. Allowing visual media to become a catalyst to prayer will encourage more people to pray, and to pray in ways that help them build a stronger relationship with God.

You may also begin to ask yourself, "Am I praying?" every time you encounter a film or television show. The answer to that is both yes and no. Doing the prayer practices with media clips on a regular basis will most likely create a new awareness that will begin to move into all of your media experiences. However, just because you once prayed with a film clip and then find yourself once again sitting in front of a film

does not make the experience a prayer. As soon as we label everything in our lives as a prayer, we tend to lose the meaning of intentional prayer. In short, be intentional about these practices.

When you watch a film or a favorite television show, be open to moments that you may want to return to later in prayer. If you are videotaping, you can return to that moment for a recap. Or, perhaps after watching a film with friends, ask them the *examen* questions in conversation. You may notice how the conversation intentionally turns into prayerful reflection.

Pay careful attention to the chapter on imageless prayer. Get away from the world of produced images from time to time and be in silence, perhaps solitude, with God. Use your experiences with visual images in prayer to help you discern what your media diet needs to be. Allow God to teach you what is the healthy and appropriate amount of time for you to spend in front of a screen. Our lives have to be about much more than watching other people's stories.

Note

1. Centering prayer is the form promoted by Thomas Keating and Basil Pennington; John Main created Christian meditation. Both of these prayers use a technique similar to what is presented here and in *The Cloud of Unknowing*.

Appendix
Is It Wise to Seek God in Virtual Reality?

The Risk of "Cultural Contamination"

For many people, just seeing the title of this book will be enough to raise both their anxiety level and blood pressure. The idea that God can be seen and sought in the movies, popular music, or television will strike them as "New Age," evil, or, at the very least, severely misguided. It will raise fears that the gospel will be compromised, that the church will be replaced by the culture of the world, and that the experience of God will be missed altogether.

These are real and reasonable fears that we want to address. First we want to offer a deeper explanation as to why we think it is possible to discern the God of Jesus Christ in modern media. Second, we wish to offer some guidelines by which to tell if the use of media is compatible with an authentic expression of the church.

Seeing the Unseen God

The Bible tells us that we cannot see the face of God and live (Exod 33:20). We are also commanded to worship God alone, and not "to make for [ourselves] an idol, whether in the form of anything that is heaven above or that is on the earth beneath" (Exod 20:4). These two commands present the people of God with a great challenge: If we worship a God we cannot see, and we cannot create graven images of

79

the God we worship, then how do we know that we are really worshiping God?

Scripture meets this challenge in a number of ways. One is through worship that uses current cultural forms in ways that point toward a God beyond form and substance. In the Old Testament, we read about Jacob pouring oil on a rock pillar that he built to honor God (Gen 28:18). David offered grains and animals in ritual sacrifice (1 Chr 21:26). Solomon built and dedicated the temple for worship (1 Kgs 8:1-14). These are examples of cultural practices used to tell both God and the people that they were worshiping and pleasing YHWH.

In the New Testament, we read about other sets of cultural practices being used to worship God. Early Christians gathered to pray and break bread together (Acts 2:43-46), were baptized with water (Acts 2:41), and professed their faith (Acts 4:2). Through these actions, early Christians found assurance that they were worshiping the God of Jesus.

Another way that the people of God knew that they were worshiping the invisible God was by following the law of God. If the people lived out their lives in certain ways as they followed God's commands, then they knew that they were living out a life that was of God and not of the world. In the same way, Jesus always attempted to clarify the true meaning of the law of God, so that people would know how best to follow God (John 13:35).

Finally, the people of God knew that they worshiped and knew the one God as they came to understand the Word of God, the revelation of God in Scripture, and, most important, the revelation of God in Jesus Christ. By coming to

hear God's words and then by entering into a faith-filled relationship with Jesus, the people of God gained confidence that they were in relationship with a God they could not see.

As we look at these solutions to the problem of worshiping an invisible God, we arrive at several conclusions important to our exploration of God in media.

---

1. The intention of the one worshiping or approaching God matters greatly in the process of coming to know God.

When Peter sought to explain to the crowd what has happened in the healing of the lame man, he desired to make known the God of Abraham, Isaac, and Jacob (Acts 3). Peter could have taken the credit for himself or told the people to worship him, but he insisted on taking no credit for the healing. Instead, he directed people's attention to the God revealed through Jesus.

The importance of this intentional search for the one God is repeated throughout Scripture. In fact, the basic prophetic message of the Old Testament is that the people were not searching for the true God, and that was their gravest sin. The very heart of idolatry is this refusal to seek God first. When we do not look for God, who is beyond the seen form, we tend to replace God with the form itself.

No matter how we worship or pray, it is essential that we clearly know our intention to seek the God of Jesus and not some other god.

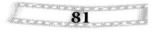

2. Our search must be grounded in the knowledge of God that comes through the revelation of Scripture.

If we tell someone that we are worshiping God, some of the obvious questions they may ask us are: "What God? What is that God like? How do you know who that God is?" The only way to answer these questions is to refer to some revelation, some unveiling of this God of ours, and that revelation is Jesus Christ as known through Scripture.

If we are not grounded in this revelation, then it does not matter what form of worship we use—we will not know who it is we are worshiping. As Jesus tells the woman at the well, we must worship in Spirit and in truth (John 4:1-42). Thus, all Christian prayer is done in reference to the God who is known through Jesus.

This grounding in revelation is often overlooked in discussions of "seeing God in all things." The mystics who contemplated God in nature, art, or service were not just experiencing some random god. They were people who lived in communities that sung and studied Scripture for several hours every day! The Word of God was indeed "very near to [them]; it is in [their] mouths and hearts for [them] to observe" (Deut 30:14).

It was out of this solid foundation that they began to pray without ceasing and came to see the true God in everything. If we could go back in time and ask them what God they were relating to, they would clearly tell you it was the God of Jesus Christ.

3. Cultural forms have always been a part of true worship, and these cultural forms change over time, as the culture changes.

The early Christians did not pile up rocks and pour oil on them as Jacob did. Nor did they slaughter sheep, burn grain, or build churches. They broke bread and devoted themselves to prayers, worshiping in a manner that was authentic and appropriate for their place and time, just as all the people in the Bible did.

This process of incorporating cultural forms into valid worship continued as the church developed. Paul used the Athenian altar to the "unknown God" as a backdrop for making his persuasive speech at the Areopagus (Acts 17:16-33). Paul knew that his audience found great meaning in that work of popular culture. Throughout the Middle Ages, stained glass windows were created not simply to be beautiful, but primarily as ways to tell biblical stories to those who could not read. Also, tunes from popular secular songs were turned into hymns after the Reformation so that people could sing God's praises to a melody they recognized.

The apostles never played a hymn on an organ. That does not mean that their worship was inadequate. It only means that the organ had not been invented yet, nor had it come to be associated with the scriptural passage, "playing on pipes and rejoicing with great joy" (1 Kgs 1:40).

The real issue behind the fear of cultural contamination is the fact that each of us becomes attached to a form of worship that "works for me," and we then come to associate

that form with "true" worship. Again, if we could travel back in time to a church in the late first century C.E., we would probably be horrified, or at least confused, by what "true" worship looked like then. We would also come to appreciate how much worship is indeed a cultural phenomenon.

Ways to Approach Praying with Media

Given the above analysis and conclusions, what can we advise as we attempt to approach God in virtual reality?

1. When conflict erupts, identify the real problem.

When someone objects to praying with modern media, it is important to clarify what is really going on. Is the problem truly a theological one about allowing in the values of the world? Or is the real problem an issue of power and control over who gets to plan worship in church?

Sorting out these basic questions is extremely important. If the issue is one of control, then perhaps what is really going on is that some people in the church are suffering as they feel a loss of the cultural forms that, for many years, have helped them relate to God. In this case, the conversation should be about managing change in your particular church. However, if the problem or issue is truly one of concern over the validity of praying with modern media, then the following discussion and reflection will be helpful.

When Elijah was fed by the ravens as he hid in the desert (1 Kgs 17:4), he did not come to the conclusion that he needed to worship ravens, even though that would have been an understandable conclusion, especially for a premodern person. Rather, he realized that the true God was using the ravens to help him. He came to this realization because his deepest desire and intention was to follow the real God.

When we approach media as a vehicle for prayer, it is important that we, too, have the same desire and intention. We need to recognize that it is possible that we are only using God as an excuse to watch *Friends*; and we need to clarify for ourselves, and our church, our true motives and intentions.

This process of discernment is necessary no matter what cultural forms we use for prayer because idolatry is the most prevalent value of the world, and it lurks in every fiber of our being. We can turn anything into a false god, be it the bulletin, the order of worship, the choir, or our favorite hymn. In the practice of prayer, we must always bring ourselves back to the basic instruction of Scripture, which tells us that we are to love *God* with all our heart, not an idol of bronze or silver, not a cultural ideal such as success or patriotism, and certainly not any electronic image.

2. Ground all prayer in the God of Jesus Christ.

Before you can see God in all things, you must first know who God is. Plopping yourself down in front of the TV and

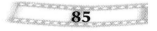

saying you are praying—without ever picking up the Bible, going to church, or receiving some instruction about the faith—is not what we are recommending in this book. The use of media in prayer, worship, youth group, adult education, or elsewhere is not an end in itself. It must be a means towards a relationship with Jesus.

This is one of the best tests to determine whether any form of worship is authentic: Does it point to itself, or does it point to the God we know in Jesus Christ? On the one hand, if your church is using media because it attracts more young adults, increases worship attendance in general, or for some other result, then this may not be an authentic expression of the gospel, and you may be conforming to the values of the world. On the other hand, if your use of media is genuinely increasing the faith in God of those extra people attending your services, then this may indeed be a sign that you are using a modern cultural form for authentic prayer.

3. Test the experience.

Our final words of guidance relate to the issue of the experience of God and the concern that somehow praying with media will limit or distort this experience. Because we are human and all experience of God is filtered through our minds and bodies, this experience will always be highly subjective and conditioned by our backgrounds and cultural experiences. Someone who has lived for fifty years with a highly structured style of worship, using words and a pipe organ, may indeed never fully experience God through movies. On the other hand, this does not rule out

an experience of God through media for someone else. Again, the solution lies in returning to Scripture to determine what it means to be in authentic relationship with God.

The witness of the New Testament defines the sign of an authentic relationship with the God of Jesus Christ as the reception of the Holy Spirit. The Spirit blessed Jesus at his baptism (Matt 3:13). Jesus breathed the Spirit onto his disciples after resurrection (John 20:22). At Pentecost, the Spirit was given to the church (Acts 2:1-13). If we take these examples of reception of the Spirit as a normative sign of an authentic relationship with God, then we can look for signs of the Spirit in a person of God.

Although the Bible includes many descriptions of a Spirit-filled life, the clearest list is given by Paul in his letter to the Galatians, in which he lists the fruit of the Spirit: "love, joy, peace, patience, kindness, generosity, faithfulness, gentleness, and self control" (Gal 5:22-23). Taking this list and applying it to our prayer with media, and to our prayer life in general, helps us assess whether or not our prayer life is authentic.

On the one hand, if prayer with media simply turns us into self-centered couch potatoes with no interest in others or service to our faith community, then we can conclude that this sort of prayer is not prayer at all. On the other hand, if our praying with media makes us more loving, generous, service-oriented people who desire to follow Jesus into the mission field, then we can conclude with equal certainty that this sort of prayer brings us into relationship with the living God.

Conclusion

We realize that we write this book in the midst of a storm of controversy and change within the church. We hope that these brief guidelines and discussions are helpful in sorting through some of the issues that you may face as you enter into what may be a radical step of praying with the narratives of popular culture.

We would never presume to declare this the best or only way to pray, nor would we say it is for everyone. But, for some people, even for many people, it is an avenue to God, and it will encourage openness to meeting God.

We have prayed using these practices. We have observed how they have been beneficial in our lives and in the lives of other Christians. Convinced it is biblically sound and spiritually enriching, we are confident that if you engage in this practice with the intention of meeting the risen Christ, you will join those throughout the centuries who have endeavored to find God in all things.